Ride The Lightning

As recorded by METALLICA on ELEKTRA RECORDS

Management: Q Prime, Inc.
Arranged by Steve Gorenberg
Music Engraving by W.R. Music
Production Manager: Daniel Rosenbaum
Art Direction: Alisa Hill
Director of Music: Mark Phillips

Photography by Ross Halfin/Vereecke

FIGHT FIRE WITH FIRE

Words and Music by
James Hetfield, Lars Ulrich, and
Cliff Burton

Additional Lyrics

2. Blow the universe into nothingness.
Nuclear warfare shall lay us to rest. *(To Chorus)*

3. Time is like a fuse, short and burning fast.
Armageddon is here, like said in the past. *(To Chorus)*

4. Soon to fill our lungs, the hot winds of death.
The gods are laughing, so take your last breath. *(To Chorus)*

FOR WHOM THE BELL TOLLS

Words and Music by
James Hetfield, Lars Ulrich
and Cliff Burton

1st, 2nd Verses
w/Rhy. Fig. 1 (2 times)

1. Make his fight on the hill in the ear-ly day.
2. Take a look to the sky just be-fore you die.

Con-stant chill deep in-
It's the last time he

side.
will.

Shout-ing gun, on they run through the end-less grey.
Black-ened roar, mas-sive roar fills the crum-bling sky.

On they fight, for they're right.__ Yes, but who's to say?
Shat-tered goal fills his soul__ with a ruth-less cry.

For a hill men would
Stran-ger now are his

kill. Why? They do not know.
eyes to this mys-ter-y.

Suf-fered wounds test their pride.
Hears the si-lence so loud.

Men of five, still a-live__ through the rag-ing glow.
Crack of dawn, all is gone ex-cept the will to be.

Gone in-sane from the pain__
Now they see what will be,__

Chorus
w/Rhy. Fig. 2 (2 times)

__ that they sure-ly know..⌐
__ blind-ed eyes to see.__⌐

For whom the bell__ tolls.__

To Coda

Time march-es on
w/Riff B (3 times)

for whom the bell__ tolls._____

Not in strict time
w/Bells

1.
B5

2.
B5

D.S. al Coda

Coda

Repeat and fade

Riff B

P.M. -

5

ESCAPE

Words and Music by
James Hetfield, Lars Ulrich
and Kirk Hammett

One_ with my mind, they_ just can't see._

No_ need to hear things_ that they say._

Life's_ for my own to live_ my own way._

See them try to bring the ham - mer down. (end half time feel)

No damn chains can hold me to the ground.

Life's_ for my own to live_ my own way._

Rhy. Fig. 3

THE CALL OF KTULU

Music by James Hetfield,
Lars Ulrich, Cliff Burton
and Dave Mustaine

9

CREEPING DEATH

Words and Music by
James Hetfield, Lars Ulrich,
Cliff Burton and Kirk Hammett

Coda   B5   C#5   F#5   E5   F5/C

Play 6 times

I'm creep-ing death.__

(Sing 1st time only)

w/Rhy. Fig. 1

w/Rh y. Fig. 2

Free time

grad. rit.

Additional Lyrics

2. Now, let my people go, land of Goshen.
   Go, I will be with thee, bush of fire.
   Blood running red and strong down the Nile.
   Plague. Darkness three days long, hail to fire. *(To Chorus)*

3. I rule the midnight air, the destroyer.
   Born. I shall soon be there, deadly mass.
   I creep the steps and floor, final darkness.
   Blood. Lamb's blood, painted door, I shall pass. *(To Chorus)*

RIDE THE LIGHTNING

Words and Music by
James Hetfield, Lars Ulrich,
Cliff Burton and Dave Mustaine

Additional Lyrics

2. Wait for the sign
   To flick the switch of death.
   It's the beginning of the end.
   Sweat, chilling cold,
   As I watch death unfold.
   Consciousness my only friend.
   My fingers grip with fear.
   What am I doing here? *(To Chorus)*

3. Time moving slow.
   The minutes seem like hours.
   The final curtain call I see.
   How true is this?
   Just get it over with.
   If this is true, just let it be.
   Wakened by horrid scream.
   Freed from this frightening dream. *(To Chorus)*

FADE TO BLACK

Words and Music by
James Hetfield, Lars Ulrich
Cliff Burton and Kirk Hammett

Bridge
w/Rhy. Fig. 2

1. No one but me can save my-self but it's too late.____
2. Yes-ter-day seems as though it nev-er ex-ist-ed.____

Now I can't think, think why I should e-ven___ try.____
Death greets me warm, now I will just say good - bye.____

2nd time to Coda II

w/Rhy. Fig. 2

D.S. al Coda II

Coda II

Repeat and fade

TRAPPED UNDER ICE

Words and Music by
James Hetfield, Lars Ulrich
and Kirk Hammett

Additional Lyrics

2. Crystalized as I lay here and rest.
   Eyes of glass stare directly at death.
   From deep sleep I have broken away.
   No one knows, no one hears what I say. *(To Chorus)*

3. No release from my cryonic state.
   What is this? I've been stricken by fate.
   Wrapped up tight, cannot move, can't break free.
   Hand of doom has a tight grip on me. *(To Chorus)*

TABLATURE EXPLANATION

TABLATURE: A six-line staff that graphically represents the guitar fingerboard. By placing a number on the appropriate line, the string and fret of any note can be indicated. For example:

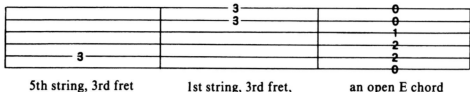

5th string, 3rd fret

1st string, 3rd fret,
2nd string, 3rd fret,
played together

an open E chord

Definitions for Special Guitar Notation (For both traditional and tablature guitar lines)

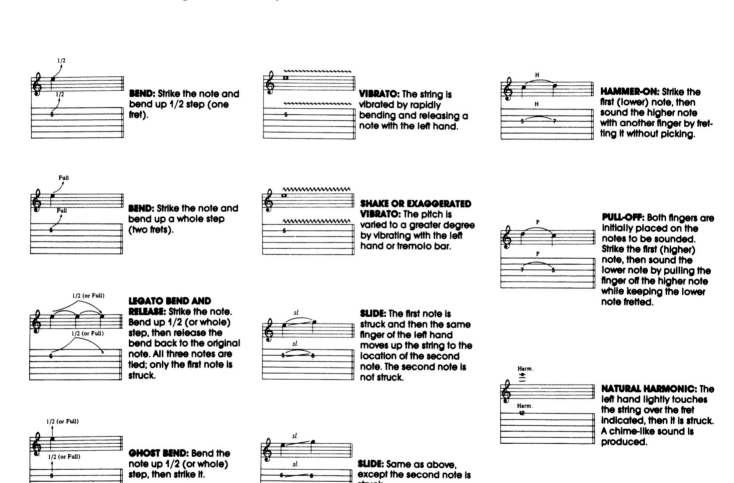

BEND: Strike the note and bend up 1/2 step (one fret).

BEND: Strike the note and bend up a whole step (two frets).

LEGATO BEND AND RELEASE: Strike the note. Bend up 1/2 (or whole) step, then release the bend back to the original note. All three notes are tied; only the first note is struck.

GHOST BEND: Bend the note up 1/2 (or whole) step, then strike it.

GHOST BEND AND RELEASE: Bend the note up 1/2 (or whole) step. Strike it and release the bend back to the original note.

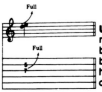

UNISON BEND: The lower note is struck slightly before the higher. It is then bent to the pitch of the higher note. They are on adjacent strings.

VIBRATO: The string is vibrated by rapidly bending and releasing a note with the left hand.

SHAKE OR EXAGGERATED VIBRATO: The pitch is varied to a greater degree by vibrating with the left hand or tremolo bar.

SLIDE: The first note is struck and then the same finger of the left hand moves up the string to the location of the second note. The second note is not struck.

SLIDE: Same as above, except the second note is struck.

SLIDE: Slide up to the note indicated from a few frets below.

SLIDE: Strike the note and slide up an indefinite number of frets, releasing finger pressure at the end of the slide.

HAMMER-ON: Strike the first (lower) note, then sound the higher note with another finger by fretting it without picking.

PULL-OFF: Both fingers are initially placed on the notes to be sounded. Strike the first (higher) note, then sound the lower note by pulling the finger off the higher note while keeping the lower note fretted.

NATURAL HARMONIC: The left hand lightly touches the string over the fret indicated, then it is struck. A chime-like sound is produced.

PALM MUTE: The note is partially muted by the right hand lightly touching the string(s) just before the bridge.

MUFFLED STRINGS: A percussive sound is produced by laying the left hand across the strings without depressing them to the fretboard and striking them with the right hand.